A Lasting
Friendship

A Lasting Friendship

A collection of poems
Edited by Susan Polis Schutz

Blue Mountain Press ™

Boulder, Colorado

Library of Congress Number: 84-73379
ISBN: 0-88396-231-4

The following works have previously appeared in Blue Mountain Arts publications:

"A friend is," by Susan Polis Schutz. Copyright © Stephen Schutz and Susan Polis Schutz, 1981. "Our Friendship," by Susan Polis Schutz. Copyright © Stephen Schutz and Susan Polis Schutz, 1983. "One of the greatest," by Edmund O'Neill. Copyright © Blue Mountain Arts, Inc., 1983. "You have known me," and "Whatever I say," by Susan Polis Schutz. Copyright © Stephen Schutz and Susan Polis Schutz, 1984. "A Lasting Friendship," by Cammie Charles; "I hope that today," by Susie Schneider; "Today, if a smile," by Paula Lee Carrico; "Every once in a while," by Tamara Hillstrom; "May the world," by Donna Abate; "You Have Given Me . . . ," by Sharon Crist; "When we're not together," by Amy Starin; "Thank you for sharing yourself . . .," by Pat Treskot; "I've always felt," by Gail Pocus; "Friend, you are beautiful," by Laine Parsons; "We've known each other," by Denise Johnston; "I used to think," by Sally J. Ethier; and "The hardest part," by Deanna Beisser. Copyright © Blue Mountain Arts, Inc., 1984. "Because you are my friend," by Sunny Mann; "I Will Always Be Here for You," by Dawn McCoy; "A Prayer for a Friend," by Rhoda-Katie Hannan; "The Greatest of Gifts," by Andrew Tawney; "Everyone needs someone," by Glenna Place; "Deep down inside . . . ," by Laine Parsons; and "I don't ever want to lose touch," by Sharon Johnson. Copyright © Blue Mountain Arts, Inc., 1985. All rights reserved.

Thanks to the Blue Mountain Arts creative staff.

ACKNOWLEDGMENTS appear on page 62.

Manufactured in the United States of America
First printing: January, 1985

Blue Mountain Press INC.

P.O. Box 4549, Boulder, Colorado 80306

CONTENTS

A Lasting Friendship

Some people are fortunate enough
to meet someone special in their lives
who, even though they each may follow
their separate ways, continue to share
a lasting friendship. . .

The special times spent together,
the people and places shared,
are memories both will always have.

They are the people remembered always,
who live in the heart no matter what . . .
always just a thought or a phone call away,
even if the years have come between.

This is for you, my special friend,
given with a special kind of love.

Thank you for all the times in my life
you were such a vital part of,
and for being the unique essence
    of our lasting friendship.

— Cammie Charles

You have known me
in good and
bad times
You have seen me
when I was happy
and when I was sad
You have listened to me
when what I said was
    intelligent
and when I talked nonsense
You have been with me
when we had fun
and when we were miserable
You have watched me
laugh
and cry
You have understood me
when I knew what I was
    doing
and when I made mistakes
Thank you for
believing in me
for supporting me
and for always being ready
to share thoughts together
You are a perfect friend

— Susan Polis Schutz

Because you
   are my friend,
   we have shared
the secrets in our lives
   and grown strong.

Because you are my friend,
   we have sealed a bond
   that time cannot remove
and smiled a secret smile that
the world shall never understand.

Because having such a friend
   is more precious than gold . . .
I have riches in untold measure
   and a heart outside my own
      to call home.

— Sunny Mann

I Will Always Be Here for You

We seem to spend our lives
planning for the future . . .
tomorrow is always in our thoughts,
while today slips away,
and yesterday sometimes returns
to remind us of our mistakes.
We try to hold the special moments,
forgetting that the best is yet to come;
that tomorrow is another day,
another chance to take,
another dream to fulfill.
Relationships don't always succeed,
friendships sometimes change,
but I want you to know,
no matter what else happens to us . . .

I will always be here for you.
Open arms to hold you,
an open heart to love you,
an open mind to listen.
You will never be alone.
Together we'll create new dreams
and take our chances.
If we fail, we won't hurt so badly,
because a friend's caring love
heals all wounds, no matter
how deep or painful.
So give me a smile that I can return,
a moment that we can share.
Allow me the time
to know you completely,
and I will always love you
just the way you are.

— Dawn McCoy

A Prayer for a Friend

This I pray for you, my friend —
That you strive to be all that you can be,
    yet never become a copy of another
That you realize your own unique qualities,
    and all that makes you special
That you open your eyes to the beauty
    in each day
That you reach out to others less fortunate
    than you
That, by giving, you learn the joy of
    receiving . . .

That you let go of the sadness of the past,
    yet always remember the good moments
That you learn to accept life as it is,
    even with its problems and disappointments
For life is meant to be enjoyed
    and, at times, endured, but never taken
    for granted
And I pray that you will be aware at all
    times that you are one special person,
    among all special persons
And do the best you can.

— Rhoda-Katie Hannan

I hope that today
and always
the love I have for you
is reaching out
and touching you —
making your days
a little brighter
and your heart
a little warmer.

I hope that today
and always
you are aware of how
special you are to me,
and how lucky I feel
to have you in my life.

— Susie Schneider

Today, if a smile
    comes to you,
a happy smile
    that perhaps you
can't explain . . .

It's because,
    in that moment,
I am thinking of you —
    and smiling, too!

— Paula Lee Carrico

I ask myself
why I have been
    blessed with someone
    so understanding
    and so caring . . .
Perhaps it's because
I can truly appreciate you
or maybe it's because
    God knew
    I needed you
    so much.

— Jean Therese

One of the greatest joys in my life
is our friendship . . . I don't think
either of us suspected, when we first
met, that we would stand where we
do today, sharing the close harmony
of our abiding friendship. But we
grew together through the days,
sharing laughter and tears, thoughts
and silence — all the things that
have become an unforgettable part
of who we are. You have always
encouraged me to share myself fully —
my hopes, my dreams . . .

my secret pains and sadnesses
that I have come to understand
better in the light of your
concerned understanding. I hope
I have reflected back to you, if
only in a small way, something
of the same. No one knows what
path tomorrow will find us walking;
but together or apart, I know
that I've found in you
the lifetime friend I have always
wished for, and that
the years passing will never change,
but only strengthen,
our enduring relationship.

— Edmund O'Neill

Every once in a while
I feel the urge to thank you . . .
not for any one particular reason,
but for everything . . .

for listening while
   I empty my troubled heart,
for not judging the little
   absurdities in this
   character of mine,
and for sharing laughter
   toward the simple things
        in life.

Today I feel the urge to thank you . . .
   not for any one particular reason,
but for everything
   you are to me.

Thank you,
   my friend.

— Tamara Hillstrom

The Greatest of Gifts

There are many stars in the sky of friendship,
but there are none that shine as brightly
for me . . . as you. You are the dearest of all,
shining high above the rest, lighting up my
life and giving me a wonderful knowledge.
I've got a friend.

Knowing that you are my friend, and always
will be, keeps my faith in happiness alive.
Whether you know it or not, you have gotten
me over many rough times. For me, I know
that things may go wrong and the world may
treat me unfairly every now and then, but
   I'll be okay.
I've got a friend who understands. . .

Your friendship is one of the things
I treasure most in life, for it gives to me
a value beyond wealth, and a wealth
beyond words.

I've wanted to express my heart's thanks,
  and if the words could be found,
    I would tell you this . . .

that come what may, I will always
consider your friendship
as the greatest of gifts.

— Andrew Tawney

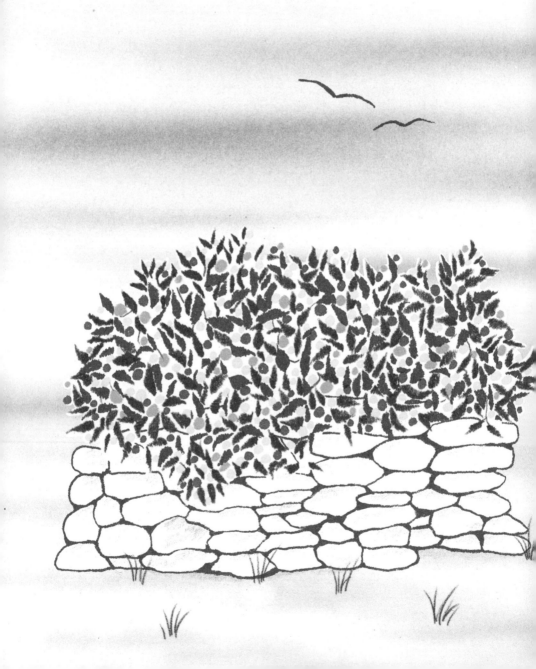

May the world
  hug you today
With its warmth and love
And whisper a joyful tune
In your heart
And may the wind
  carry a voice
That tells you
  there is a friend
Sitting in another corner
  of the world
Right now
Wishing you well.

— Donna Abate

My Friend

Your specialness is wrapped in the
    colors of the rainbow,
and my thoughts of you blaze with
    sunlight.
Outstretched and open, your hands
    reach out to me,
and I marvel at how much you willingly
    and graciously give of yourself.

You listen carefully, grasping every
shade of meaning from my spoken
    thoughts.
You permit me an openness of expression
    without judging or accusing.

You behold and accept me in all facets
    of my being,
and you have earned my trust and
    admiration.

Your confidence in me is a mountain
    of inspiration . . .

spurring me on to climb to my own
   heights of possibilities.

With you, there are no expectations
   to meet.
I enjoy the privilege of being
   completely at ease with you,
since you allow me to unlock and
   free the real me.

I feel secure in our friendship
because you never turn away from me.
Your ever-present concern and devotion
   overwhelm me;
your trust and love humble me;
your presence blesses me.

You are the definition of the word
"friend"
and the superlative of all friends.

— Lenore Turkeltaub

Whatever I say
means more when
you listen
Whatever I think
means more when
you understand
Whatever I do
means more when
you are there
Whatever happens to me
means more if
I can share it with you
Thank you for
adding so much
to my life

— Susan Polis Schutz

You Have
Given Me . . .

Strength to know myself
Hope that my life could be better
Kindness when I was hurting
Refuge when I was frightened
Solace for my grief
Faith when I despaired
Options when I felt trapped
Comfort when I was alone
Understanding when I
    was confused
Challenge for me to change
Patience when I balked
Support when I tried
Acceptance when I failed
Encouragement to go on . . .

Warmth to sustain me
Insight to better comprehend
Knowledge for growth
Recognition of my
    accomplishments
Guidance toward higher goals
And through all of these,
    an example that will sustain
    and nurture the person
    I am becoming.

        Thank you for caring.

                            — Sharon Crist

My friend,
if I could give you
one thing,
I would give you
the ability to see
yourself
as others see you . . .
then you would realize
what a truly special
person
you are.

— Barbara A. Billings

Dear Friend . . .

You helped me to get in touch
with who I am . . .
and encouraged me
  to be better.

You motivated me
to overcome my fears,
and you were more proud than I
  when I succeeded.

You respected
my thoughts and opinions
and taught me to feel
they were worthwhile
— and worth expressing. . .

And although I doubt
that I could ever give
as much as you have given . . .

I sincerely want you to feel
you can call on me
　　whenever you need to.

You've come through for me
so many times . . .
Now it is my turn
　　to come through for you.

　　　　　　　　　— Paula Finn

When we're
not together . . .

It isn't just your friendship
   that I miss . . .
It isn't the time we spent
   together
or the fun we had . . .
I miss the trust and the
   understanding,
the giving and the sharing,
the peaceful companionship,
the silence and the noise
   of us . . .
I miss everything
   about you.

— Amy Starin

Everyone needs someone like you . . .

Even though I'm in control of my life —
perhaps not doing exactly what I want
to do, but working in that direction —
sometimes I get scared. So caught up
and overwhelmed by the world around
me that I want to run away and hide.

Then I remember what you taught me . . .
That security comes from within, and
the strength you lend to others will
be there for you when you need it.
You never told me in words; I learned
it just by being around you.

With that in mind, I don't get scared
very often anymore. But when I do,
I'm so glad that I'm one of the lucky
ones . . . Not everyone has someone
    like you.

— Glenna Place

I couldn't care about
   a person
any more than I care
   about you.
I couldn't find a better
   friend if I searched
the world over.
I couldn't trust anyone
   any more than I trust
      you.
You are my friend,
   in a very special way.

— Rick Norman

Our Friendship

We have formed
a friendship
that has become
invaluable to me
We discuss our goals
and plan our future
We express our fears
and talk about our dreams...

We can be very serious
or we can just have fun
We understand each other's lives
and try to encourage each other
in all that we do
We have formed
a friendship
that makes our lives
so much
nicer

— Susan Polis Schutz

Dear friend,
you've stepped outside
and stood beside me
long enough to feel the cold,
hear the thunder,
and see the lightning
contained in my every storm.

You've looked at me
with understanding,
while your smile has transmitted
the warmth I so needed,
even when your lips were silent. . .

Your eyes have met mine,
accepting the challenge
that true friendship calls for;
they have been a window
for me to gently read within you
what you care to let me know.

We've never needed empty words
or fill-in phrases,
for together, my friend,
we have built the foundation
needed for a lifetime friendship,
which we now hold so dear.

— Elizabeth Torres

Thank you for sharing yourself . . .

It started with a simple hello,
But as time passed we
Started talking more and more,
Learning a little each time.
You listened to all my feelings. . .

And I learned about yours,
Not knowing then how
Close we would become.
Now through our talks
We not only learn
How much we have in common,
But also that we'll be there
For each other
Always.

— Pat Treskot

Deep down inside . . .

There's a person inside me
    with so many thoughts . . .
with wishes of things
    I'd someday like to do,
and fantasies of things
    that have to do with you.
Inside of me sometimes
is someone who cries now and then,
and who feels many needs that never
    quite get expressed.
Somehow . . . you know about
    these times,
and you keep me
from getting too depressed
            about things.
You know me so well . . .

you have a wonderful knack
    for calling at just the right time,
touching just the right place,
    saying just the right words . . .

Everyone else only knows
    the "outside" of me . . .
        it's only from you that
    I feel I don't need to hide.

It's with love and honesty and gratitude
    that I tell you now . . . that
you're the only one
who has ever really known me . . .
        deep down inside.

— Laine Parsons

I've always felt that you
accept me as I am.
Patiently, you've waited quietly
with me while I listened
   to myself.
Yet there were other times, too,
when you showed that you have
the sensitivity and perception
to know when to challenge me
and actively encourage me . . .

You dared me to think deeply,
to feel honestly,
to speak directly.
I discovered a great joy
in trusting you
with the knowledge
        you have of me.

You are a special person
        in my life.

— Gail Pocus

Friend, you are
beautiful . . . all over

It is absolutely wonderful to have
someone in your life who is caring
and giving and gracious — someone whose
smiles are like sunshine and laughter
and whose words always seem to say
the things you most like to hear . . .
because those magical people are really
beautiful . . . inside.

And it is a special privilege to know
someone whose outward appearance . . .

is a delight just to see — someone who
lights up a room with radiance and
who lights up my little corner of the
world with a loveliness it has never
known before . . . because special people
like that are really beautiful . . . outside.

But most of all, it is one of the
world's most special blessings to
have a person in your life who can
add so much pleasure and such magnificence
to the days — as you have to mine . . .
because you're someone who is beautiful . . .
                    all over.

                    — Laine Parsons

A friend is
someone who is concerned
with everything you do

A friend is
someone to call upon
during good and bad times...

A friend is
someone who understands
whatever you do

A friend is
someone who tells you
the truth about yourself

A friend is
someone who knows
what you are going through
at all times

A friend is
someone who does not
compete with you

A friend is
someone who is genuinely happy
for you when things go well

A friend is
someone who tries to
cheer you up when
things don't go well

A friend is
an extension of yourself
without which
you are not complete

Thank you for being my friend

— Susan Polis Schutz

We've known each other
for a long time
Sharing our joys, our sadnesses,
our special dreams
We've grown close over this time,
And our friendship is very special.

I want to tell you just how much
your friendship means to me
And I want to give you, over and over
again
Every day . . .
The gift of my friendship
and love.

— Denise Johnston

I used to think
we chose our own friends,
but I wonder now if we
    really do . . .
For none but God could
    have chosen for me
        a friend so special
        as you.

— Sally J. Ethier

I don't ever want to lose touch
with you . . .

Once someone comes into my life,
   I can't just let them slip away.
I cannot accept that.
People are too important.
Once I care . . . I will always care.
For friends, I will always be there.
People in my past are part of my life,
part of who I am,
   and I don't want them to disappear.

Keeping in touch is important to me . . .
enough to let me know that
although we don't spend time together,
we do share some of the same
thoughts and memories.

Let's keep in touch . . . okay?

— Sharon Johnson

The hardest part of being a friend
is knowing
when you're needed a little
and when you're needed a lot.
So just in case you're in need
of a friendly "Hi" today,
I wanted
to let you know I'm here —
still caring
still thinking about you
still being your friend.

— Deanna Beisser

ACKNOWLEDGMENTS

We gratefully acknowledge the permission granted by the following authors, publishers and authors' representatives to reprint poems and excerpts from their publications.

Jean Therese for "I ask myself." Copyright © Jean Therese, 1981. All rights reserved. Reprinted by permission.

Lenore Turkeltaub for "My Friend." Copyright © Lenore Turkeltaub, 1985. All rights reserved. Reprinted by permission.

Barbara A. Billings for "My friend, if I could." Copyright © Barbara A. Billings, 1983. All rights reserved. Reprinted by permission.

Paula Finn for "Dear Friend . . ." Copyright © Paula Finn, 1985. All rights reserved. Reprinted by permission.

Rick Norman for "I couldn't care about." Copyright © Rick Norman, 1985. All rights reserved. Reprinted by permission.

Elizabeth Torres for "Dear friend, you've stepped." Copyright © Elizabeth Torres, 1985. All rights reserved. Reprinted by permission.

A careful effort has been made to trace the ownership of poems used in this anthology in order to obtain permission to reprint copyrighted materials and to give proper credit to the copyright owners.

If any error or omission has occurred, it is completely inadvertent, and we would like to make corrections in future editions provided that written notification is made to the publisher: BLUE MOUNTAIN PRESS, INC., P.O. Box 4549, Boulder, Colorado 80306.